All About

MAPS

Amazing Activity Book

Fun Facts, Mazes, Games, and Brain Teasers

Edited by
Paola Misesti

Illustrations by
Agnese Baruzzi

Happy Fox
BOOKS

MAPS
Let's Draw the World!

Geography is a fascinating subject for both children and adults alike, allowing you to discover many different aspects of the world we live in. This book mainly focuses on **cartography**, a subject that may seem difficult for children but is engaging and fun when presented in the form of a game. Thanks to the story about two young apprentices, **Gea and Tom**, children can learn the secrets of cartography by making tools, learning how to use them, and discovering spatial coordinates. This will make it possible for them to orient themselves in different places and situations. By the end of the book, they will know how to read and create different types of maps.

Page by page, children will learn about the **different types of maps and their purposes**. They will discover how to orient themselves through the **use of spatial coordinates and a few navigational tools**, including a compass. Halfway through the book, they will learn more about the concepts of **natural and artificial features**, finding out how to represent them on a map. Finally, they will be able to put what they have learned into practice by making some maps on their own. At the end of the story, each reader will be awarded an apprentice cartographer's rosette.

While the activities are presented as fun and practical games, they also offer young readers a lot of information and knowledge on the world of cartography. At the bottom of the pages, they will also find boxes containing interesting facts.

A Few Notes About the Activities

The order of the activities is designed to allow children to acquire knowledge gradually and easily, and we recommend following the story page by page.

There is a mix of simple and complex activities, making the book engaging and stimulating for children of different ages. They will also find materials to **cut out and use for making tools**, each accompanied by detailed and illustrated explanations.

In addition to the activities, there are also eight pages of **stickers** to use in the book, and all of the solutions to the activities can be found on the last few pages.

All of the activities are designed for children to do on their own, but adult supervision and interaction is always best, especially for younger children.

Let's get ready to explore!

Hi!

My name's Gea, and I'm an aspiring geographer. I love geography and anything that has to do with studying the earth. My friend Tom, on the other hand, wants to be a cartographer. He knows absolutely everything about maps. Tom's going to be sharing loads of secrets and interesting facts in this book. We both belong to the future geographers club. If you'd like to know more about us, take a look at our membership cards.

The Future Geographers Club

FIRST NAME:	Gea
LAST NAME:	Welt
AGE:	10
HOBBIES:	Geography, reading, photography, minerals
FAVORITE ANIMAL:	Panda
FAVORITE COLOR:	Purple

The Future Geographers Club

FIRST NAME:	Tom
LAST NAME:	Compass
AGE:	11
HOBBIES:	Cartography, video games
FAVORITE ANIMAL:	Chameleon
FAVORITE COLOR:	Green

Welcome to the Club!

You can join the future geographers club, too! Fill out the membership card below, then cut it out. Now, cut out the ruler on the right; you're going to need it to measure the geo-notches in an activity! There's also an extra membership card, so why not invite someone else to join the club!

The Future Geographers Club

FIRST NAME: _____

LAST NAME: _____

AGE: _____

HOBBIES: _____

_____

FAVORITE ANIMAL: _____

FAVORITE COLOR: _____

The Future Geographers Club

FIRST NAME: _____

LAST NAME: _____

AGE: _____

HOBBIES: _____

_____

FAVORITE ANIMAL: _____

FAVORITE COLOR: _____

- 25
- 24
- 23
- 22
- 21
- 20
- 19
- 18
- 17
- 16
- 15
- 14
- 13
- 12
- 11
- 10
- 9
- 8
- 7
- 6
- 5
- 4
- 3
- 2
- 1

Geography and Its Tools

Geography is the science that studies, describes, and depicts earth's landscapes, and in order to do this it uses many tools.

Identify the objects that Gea and all other geographers use. Discover what her **favorite tool** is by writing the letters shown with the correct objects in the order you find them below.

Map **C**

Armchair **M**

Computer **O**

Candle **F**

Binoculars **M**

Camera **P**

Suitcase **R**

Sunglasses **T**

Compass **A**

Charts **S**

Hat **I**

Drone **S**

ANSWER: ___ ___ ___ ___ ___ ___ ___

The word "geography" means "a description of the earth." It originates from two greek words: geo (the earth) and graph (to write about something).

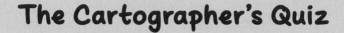

The Cartographer's Quiz

Cartography is the science of making maps of the earth's surface and features.

Maps are very important for us geographers. Let's take a quiz together to find out exactly what a cartographer does. Find the mystery word! Answer the questions and circle the letters corresponding to the correct answers. Then write the letters you circled in the answer bar above the questions. The mystery word is one of my favorite hobbies!

ANSWER: ___ ___ ___ ___

What does a cartographer use to create maps?
- photos and images .... M
- squares .... B
- songs .... F

How does a cartographer reproduce large surface areas on a map?
- by eye .... E
- by reducing the scale .... A
- with scissors I

How does a cartographer make the reader understand the things that are on the map, for example buildings or airports?
- by drawing arrows .... R
- by not indicating them with anything ... S
- with symbols and colors .... P

How does a cartographer explain what the different colors and symbols on a map mean?
- by writing the explanations in a table ... S
- by making a video .... E
- by writing a book V

What's Tom Drawing?

Tom looks very busy, but what's he doing?
You can find out by first writing the words next to the pictures, and then writing the letters with a number underneath them in the **boxes** below.

_ _ _ _ _ _ _ _ _
                  2

_ _ _ _ _ _ _
       1

_ _ _ _ _

_ _ _ _ _ _ _ _
        3

_ _ _ _ _
   4

_ _ _ _ _ _ _
       5

_ _ _ _ _

Primitive people also made maps, using stone or wood or by painting on rocks.

1	2	3	4	5

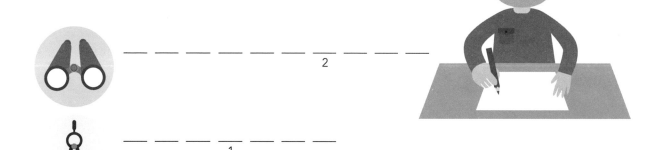

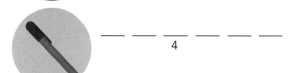

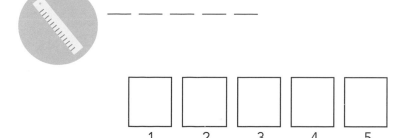

Have you ever seen any of these Maps?

We use maps every day.

Here are a few that Gea found.
Put an **X** in the box next to the ones you recognize
and write down where you've seen them.

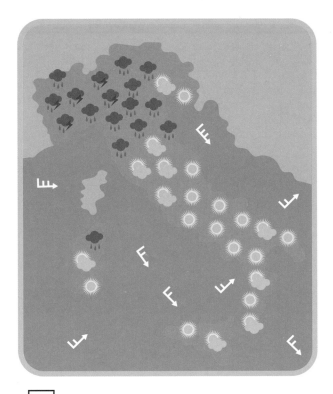

☐ _____

☐ _____

☐ _____   ☐ _____

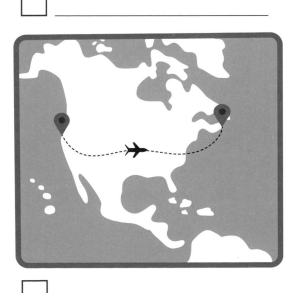

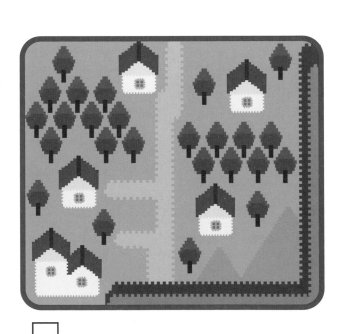

Types of Maps

There are different types of maps, and each one has its own name and purpose.

Help us to **complete them** with the stickers found at the back of the book.

Sky map: Shows the constellations.

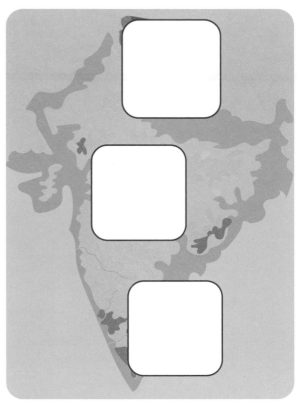

Physical map: Shows the natural features of a place (mountains, plains, rivers, lakes, etc.)

Topographic map: Shows small areas, for example, streets and squares in a city, or hiking trails.

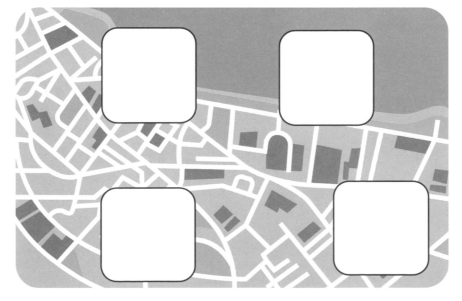

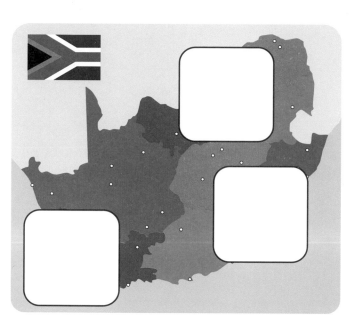

Political map: Shows borders between states, countries, and regions.

Evacuation map: Shows emergency exit routes.

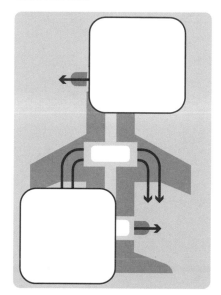

Thematic map: Shows the typical features of a place; for example, a thematic map of animals shows us which animals live in a country.

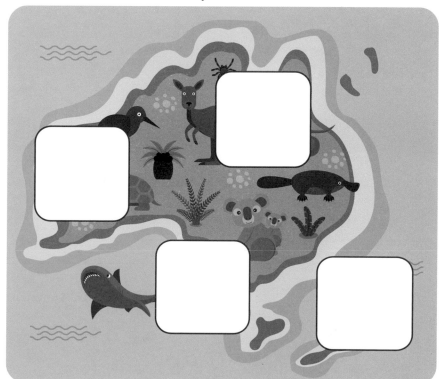

Find the Map

What a mess! The computer's erased all the data, and now some of the maps don't have a name or a description.

You can help Gea! Write the **name** of each map, using the previous activity to help you, and then use the **stickers** to find the icon that describes it.

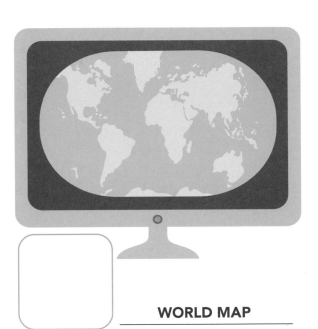

WORLD MAP

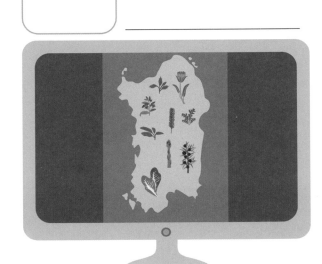

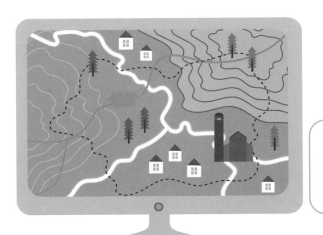

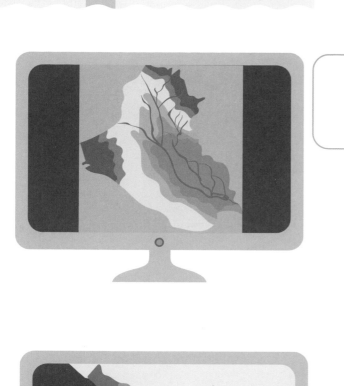

CITY MAP

Shows **natural environments**, such as rivers, mountains, and lakes.

Show **houses, buildings, and roads**.

Shows **boundaries** between states and regions, as well as all the cities.

Shows **the whole world**.

Shows lots of **details** and is often used by **hikers** and explorers.

Gives information about a **distinctive feature** of a place, such as plants, the climate, animals, or industries.

The World Map: Earth at a Glance

A world map is a special map that shows us the whole world at once.
Although it's not detailed, it's very useful because it allows us to see—among other things—just how far away other places are. Complete the map by attaching the animal stickers in the right place!

Use the **ruler** that you cut out to help Gea **measure the geo-notches** between the dots, and then answer the following questions.

How many **geo-notches** are there between ...

- Gea and the moose? _____

- Gea and the polar bear? _____

- Tom and the panda? _____

- The kangaroo and the tiger? _____

- The lion and the crocodile? _____

- The tiger and the panda? _____

- Tom and the lion? _____

- The crocodile and the penguin? _____

What's the difference between a world map and a globe? A world map shows us the whole planet on a flat piece of paper, while a globe is a spherical model of earth where we can only look at one part at a time.

Time to Go Home!

What are maps for?

Gea and I have to **find our way home** by using our maps.
Draw the path each of us needs to take. Which one of us will get home first?

Gea got home faster than I did because she had a **proper map**, making it easier for her to find her way home. The map made it easier for her to **orient** herself!

Don't Lose Your Way

Maps help us to not get lost and make it easier for us to find what we're looking for.

Help Tom draw:
• the fastest route from the **supermarket** to **Gea's house**
• the route from the **supermarket** to **Gea's house**, via the **playground**
• the route from Tom's location to **his house**, passing by the **toy shop** and **Gea's house**
Use 3 different colors.

Let's Draw a Compass Rose

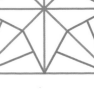

Do you know what the cardinal points are? they are special points that are always the same wherever we are in the world. Once we've identified them, we don't need anything else to orient ourselves.

There are 8 cardinal points: **north, south, east, west, northeast, southeast, southwest, and northwest**.
A **compass rose** is a simple drawing that shows us where these points are.
It's really easy to draw. Try drawing one using your ruler to help you!
Follow my examples! Then, color your compass rose and indicate the cardinal points.

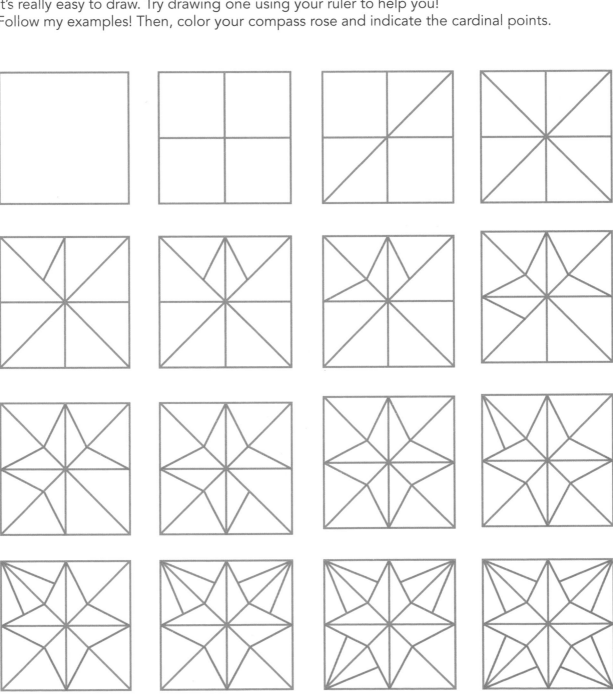

Let's Build a Special Compass

A compass is another tool that indicates the cardinal points and helps us orient ourselves.

The **magnetic needle** always points **north**. Once you know where north is, finding the other cardinal points is easy: **south** is the **opposite** of north; **west** is to the **left** of north; and **east** is to its **right**.
Gea and I use a special compass. Would you like one, too?
Cut out the dial and the needle, then attach the needle with a paper fastener.

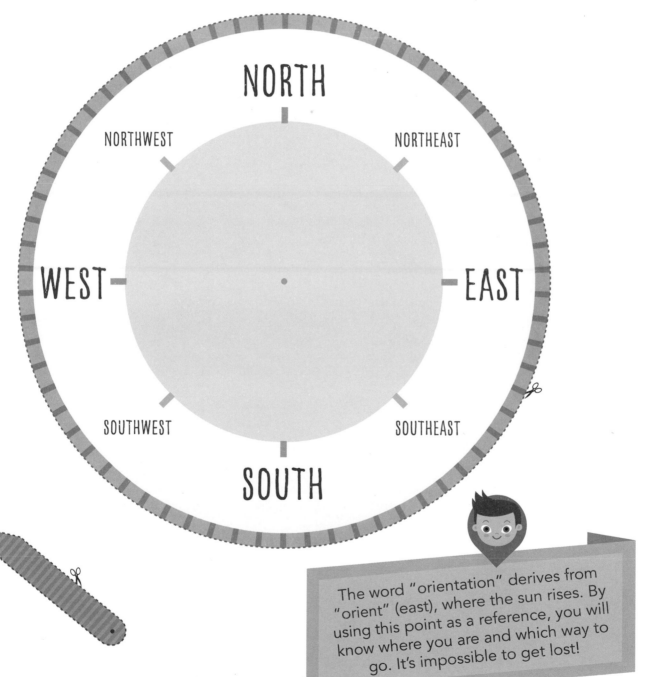

NORTH

NORTHWEST

NORTHEAST

WEST

EAST

SOUTHWEST

SOUTHEAST

SOUTH

The word "orientation" derives from "orient" (east), where the sun rises. By using this point as a reference, you will know where you are and which way to go. It's impossible to get lost!

A magnetic compass always points north. you can also find north by using our special compass.

Finding north is easy—just follow the **sun**.
Place your compass on the page, then turn the page toward where the sun rises and sets.
Remember: The sun rises in the **east**, sets in the west, and is in the **south** at noon.
Once you have oriented the page according to where the sun is, you can also orient the compass to find out where north is. Now that you know where all the cardinal points are, you can have fun figuring out which direction your bedroom or kitchen is in.

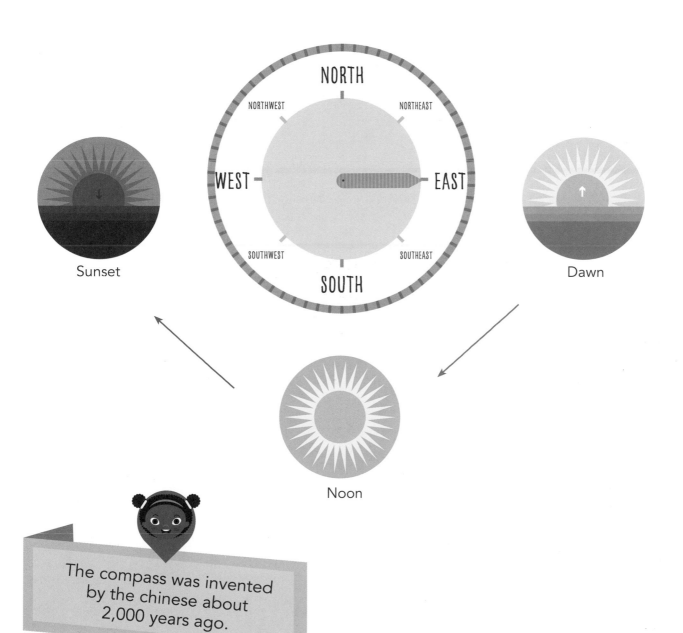

Sunset

NORTH

NORTHWEST   NORTHEAST

WEST   EAST

SOUTHWEST   SOUTHEAST

SOUTH

Dawn

Noon

The compass was invented by the chinese about 2,000 years ago.

Find the Points

Gea and I invented a really fun game.

Use your special compass to fill in the missing cardinal points on each map, and then answer Gea's questions.

Beginner's Level

Where's the hotel excelsior in relation to Gea?

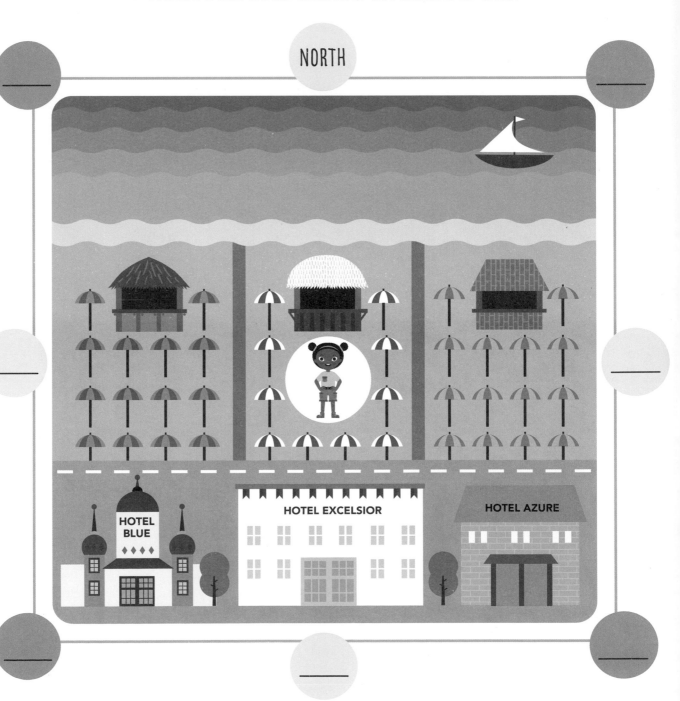

NORTH

HOTEL BLUE

HOTEL EXCELSIOR

HOTEL AZURE

Turn the needle on your compass to the same direction as the point written on the map. Now, write the missing cardinal points on the dotted lines. Can you pass all the levels and get to the "final challenge"?

Intermediate Level

Where's the airport in relation to Tom?

SOUTH

Expert Level

Where's the hospital in relation to Gea?

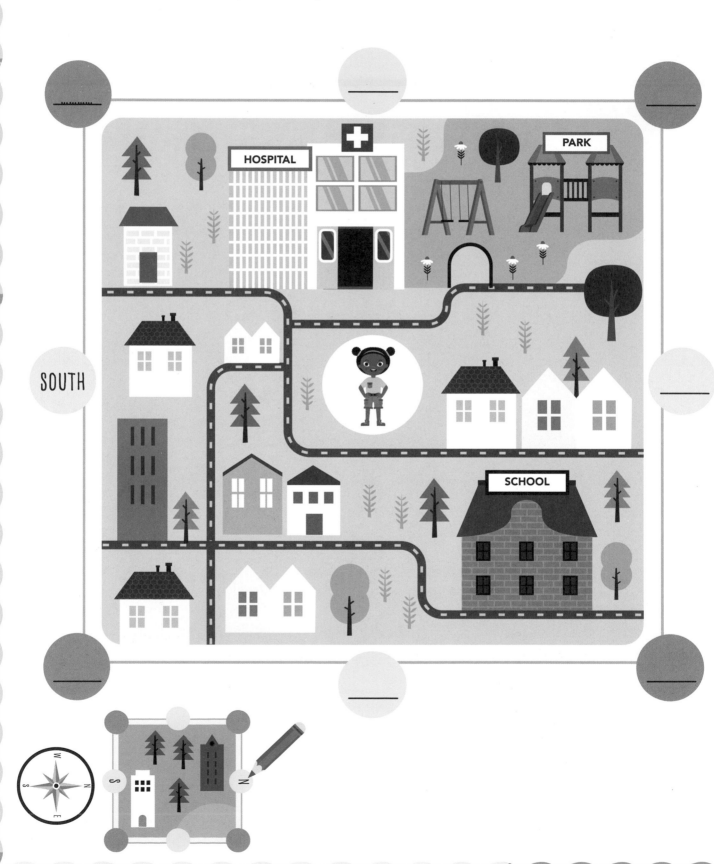

Final Challenge

Where's the tower in relation to Tom?

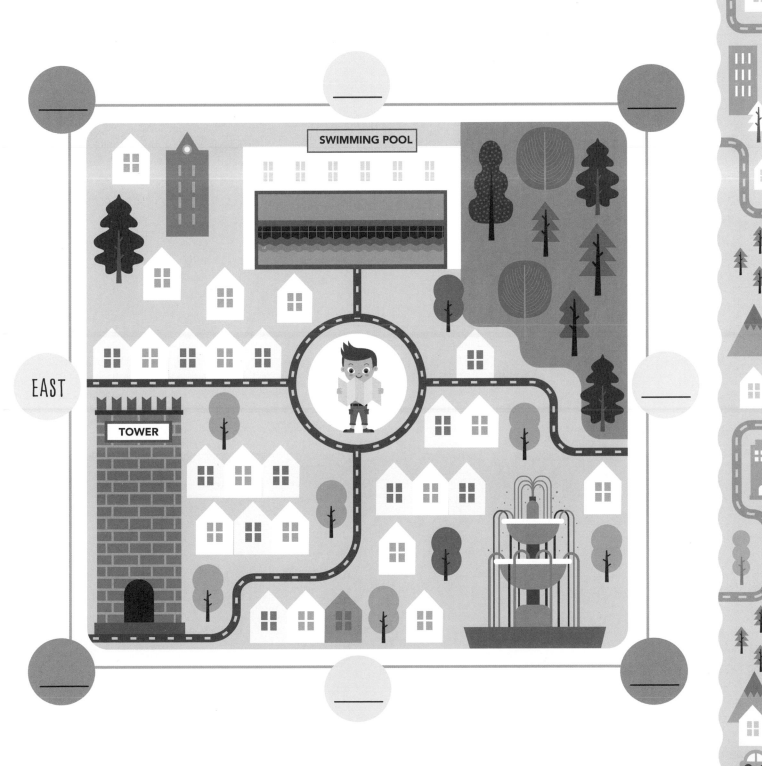

Let's Make a Real Compass

Would you like to help us make a real compass?

The needle is magnetic and will always point north.

You will need:
- an apple
- a bowl
- a needle
- a marker
- a sheet of paper
- a magnet
- water

Let's make the dial of our compass first. Place the bowl in the middle of the sheet of paper. Using the marker, write the cardinal points on the paper, around the bowl: remember that north and south are opposite each other, west is to the left of north, and east is opposite of west.

Now, let's prepare the magnetic needle that will always show us where north is. Rub the tip of the needle on the magnet at least 60 times, always in the same direction. This will magnetize the needle.

Now, cut a slice of apple, with the help of an adult. The slice must be at least 0.4 inches (1 cm) thick.

Stick the needle through the slice of apple, as shown in the drawing.

Fill the bowl with water and put the slice of apple into the bowl. Our compass is ready! The needle will start to rotate, and the tip will always end up pointing in the same direction: north. Now let's turn the dial on our paper compass so that north is in the same position indicated by the needle. What happens if we move the apple? The needle will always turn back to north!

N

W

E

S

Now, you can have fun discovering where your school, the playground, or friends' houses are!

Meridians and Parallels

Meridians and parallels are imaginary lines that we draw to orient ourselves. Do you know what they look like?

Meridians are vertical lines that divide the earth into lots of equal segments. There are **360** of them. The **0** meridian is called the **Greenwich Meridian** because it runs through a place in England called Greenwich.

Parallels are horizontal lines that form circles around the Earth. There are **180** of them. The largest circle around the center of the Earth is called the **equator**.

The meridians and parallels form a **map grid** that makes it possible for us to know where we are or where a certain place is. This simple experiment will help you understand what they look like.

You will need:

- an orange
- a blue marker
- a red marker

1

Peel the orange: this will be our Earth.

2

Draw lots of vertical lines with the blue marker, following the lines between the orange's segments. These will be the **meridians**.

3

Now, use a red marker to draw a horizontal line around the middle of the **orange**; this will be the equator. Then draw lots of circles above it and below it. These will be the **parallels**.

4

As you can see, a **grid** has now appeared on our orange-Earth, which we can use to **orient** ourselves.

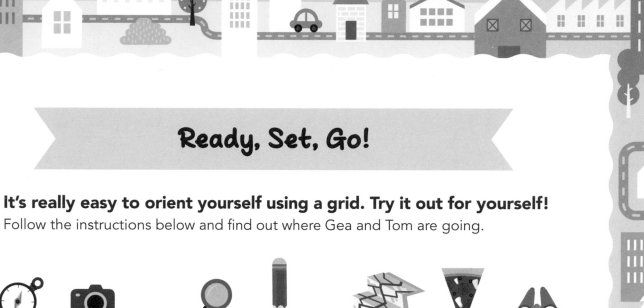

Ready, Set, Go!

It's really easy to orient yourself using a grid. Try it out for yourself!

Follow the instructions below and find out where Gea and Tom are going.

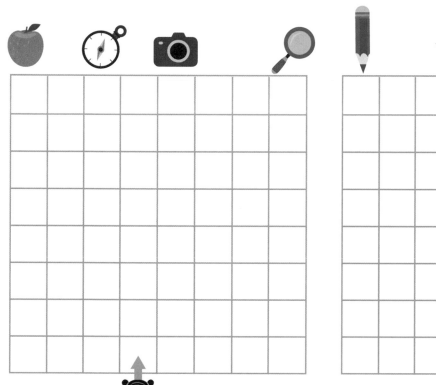

2 steps forward
4 steps to the right
3 steps forward
3 steps to the left
1 step forward
4 steps to the left
2 steps forward

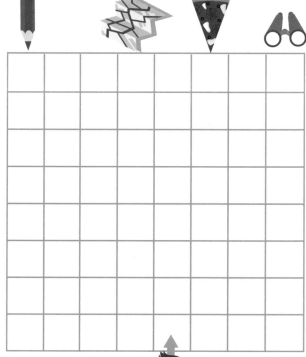

2 steps forward
3 steps to the left
3 steps forward
5 steps to the right
2 steps forward
3 steps to the left
1 step forward

**Use this grid to create
your own path!**

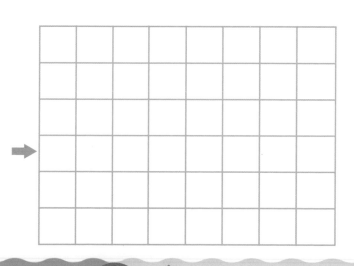

How to Use a Map Grid

A map grid, which looks just like the grids on the previous page, is made up of rows and columns. Thanks to coordinates (numbers and letters), we can use it to find a point on a plane.

It's very simple to use: We use the intersections of the rows and columns to find the square we are looking for.
Let's try it together!

The **leaf** is in C 2
The **tree** is in D 3
The **hedgehog** is in G 2
The **acorn** is in G 7
The **car** is in B 6
The **house** is in E 6.

Find the correct coordinates and help Gea answer the questions.

Where's the **flower**?
Where's the **chestnut**?
Where's the **stone**?
Where's the **mushroom**?
Where's the **ladybug**?
Where's the **tree**?
Where's the **pine cone**?

Tom has to put some animals and plants into this grid.

Follow his instructions and attach the stickers in the right place!

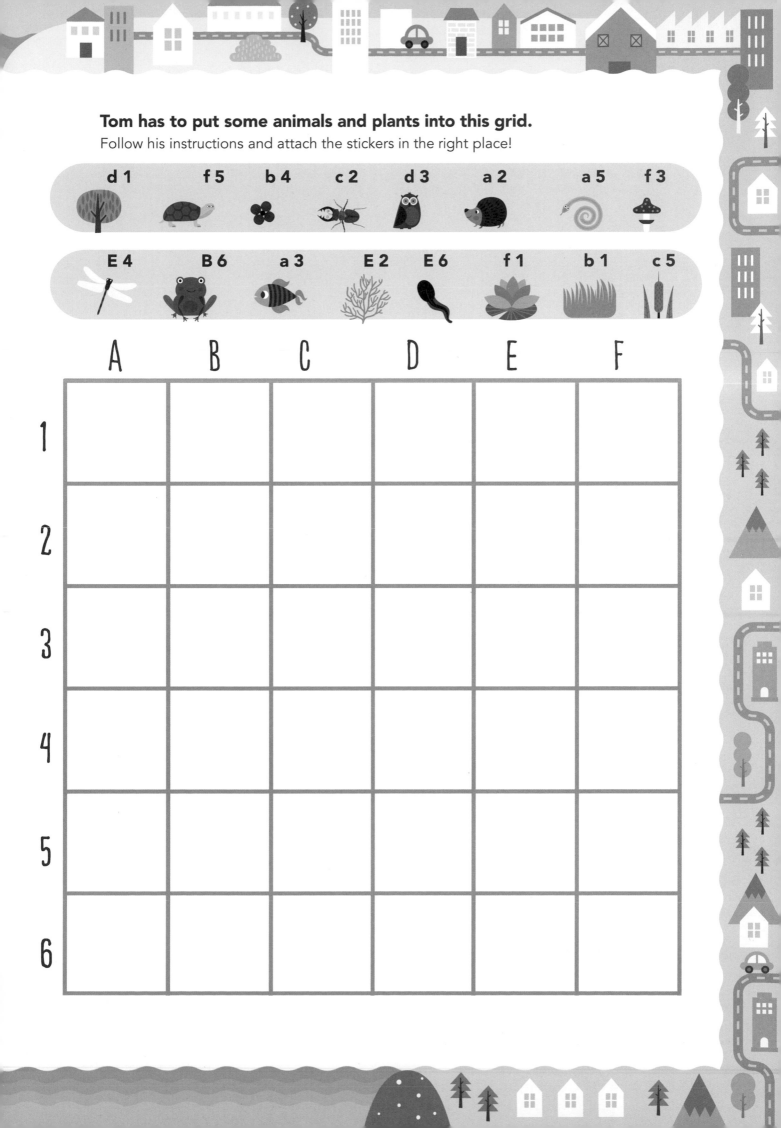

| | d 1 | f 5 | b 4 | c 2 | d 3 | a 2 | a 5 | f 3 |
| E 4 | B 6 | a 3 | E 2 | E 6 | f 1 | b 1 | c 5 |

	A	B	C	D	E	F
1						
2						
3						
4						
5						
6						

Scavenger Hunt

Play this scavenger hunt with a friend!

Find the **stickers** at the back of the book. Stick them all on a piece of cardboard, and then cut them out. Each player will have **12 tiles**, made with 12 different stickers. Place a **book** between the two pages so that your friend can't see where you put your tiles on the grid. Now, arrange your tiles on the squares of your grid.

	A	B	C	D	E	F
1						
2						
3						
4						
5						
6						

Take turns trying to guess where each other's tiles are, using the **coordinates** to help you. If your opponent guesses a tile correctly, flip it upside down.

The winner is the first person to find out where all their opponent's tiles are!

You can put the tiles anywhere you want, even really close to each other, as long as anything aquatic, like the fish or the anchor, is in the water.

All the other tiles must be on the island.

	A	B	C	D	E	F
1						
2						
3						
4						
5						
6						

Let's Scale Down

We cartographers have a problem when we have to draw a map: The surface areas we are reproducing are far, far bigger than a piece of paper.

We have to make them smaller, being careful to keep the areas in their correct **proportion**. Using map grids makes this much easier. This **method** is called "**scaling down.**" I'll show you how to do it!

First, we draw a 3x3 square grid in the middle of our map grid.

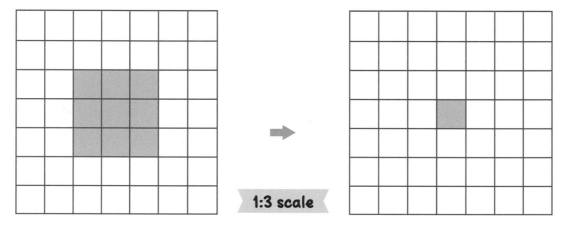

1:3 scale

Now, let's make it smaller, so that each 3-square side becomes just 1 square long; 1 square in the scaled-down picture equals 3 squares in the original one. The square now has a **scale of 1:3**. In real life, the squares represent a unit of measurement, for example, 1 foot or 1 mile.

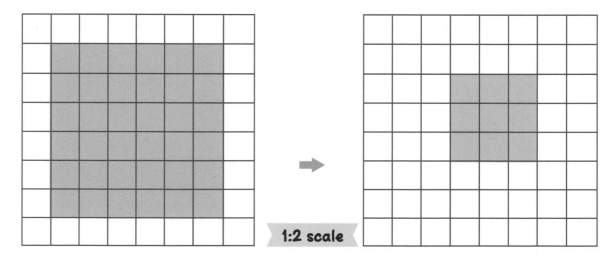

1:2 scale

In this grid, each square in the scaled-down picture represents 2 in the original one. This square now has a **scale of 1:2**.

And in this grid? How many squares of the original figure does one square of the reduced figure represent? Work out the scale!

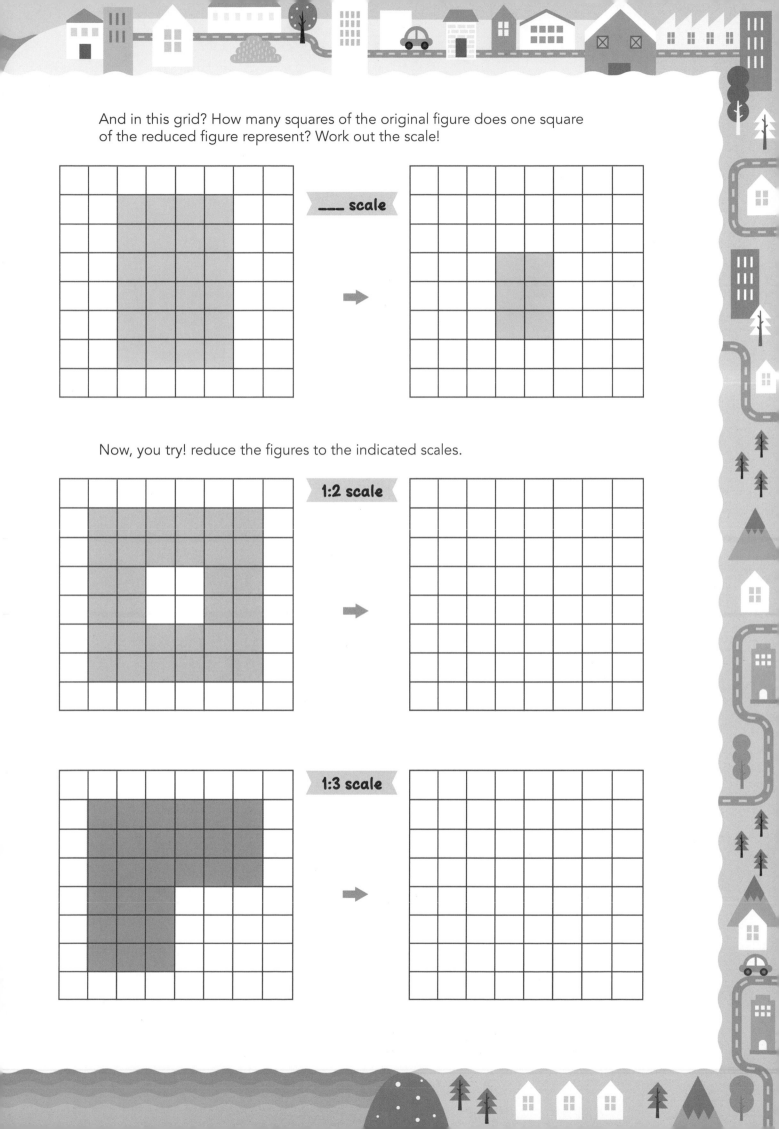

___ scale

Now, you try! reduce the figures to the indicated scales.

1:2 scale

1:3 scale

Natural and Artificial Features

A map shows both natural features, such as trees, rivers, seas, and mountains, and artificial features that have been created by humans, such as houses, factories, ports, and bridges.

Help Gea find everything on the list by circling **natural features** in **green** and **man-made features** in **red**.

River

School

Hospital

Factory

Lake

Campsite

Ice-cream parlor

Woods

Orchard

Farmland

Castle

Wind turbines

Village

Umbrellas

Natural landscapes change over time, both due to the actions of humans, who build cities and roads, and natural events, for example earthquakes and floods. Maps are also used to record these changes.

A Matter of Colors

How are natural features like rivers, oceans, mountains, and plains reproduced on a map?

On geographic maps, **colors** are used.
Darker colors indicate that a mountain is **higher** at that point or that the ocean is **deeper**.

Connect the colors on the map with what they indicate.

- VERY HIGH MOUNTAINS
- LOW MOUNTAINS
- HILLS
- PLAINs
- GLACIER
- SHALLOW OCEAN
- VERY DEEP OCEAN

Help Gea color the map with the correct colors.

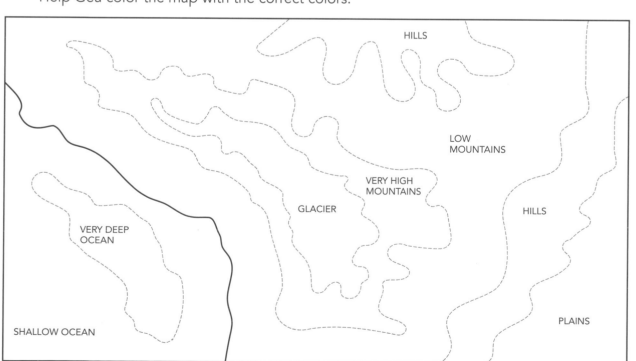

Let's Play with Pictures

in thematic maps, pictures are used to represent features that are typical of a place, such as animals, plants, crops, and industries, to name just a few.

Using the **stickers**, help Tom **complete** these thematic maps.

Thematic Map of Food

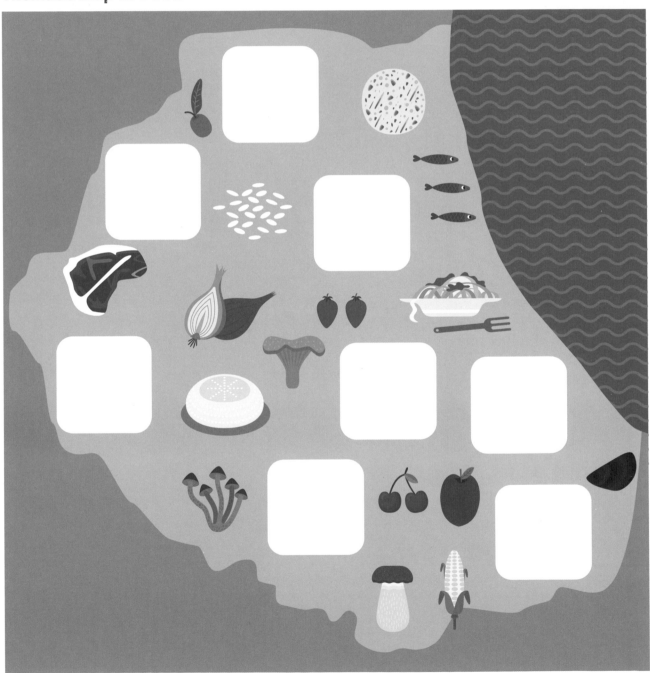

Thematic Map of Industries

Thematic Map of Animals

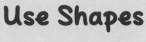

Use Shapes

In topographic maps, another way to represent mountains is by using contour lines.

A mountain with **one high peak** is represented by **lots of circles inside each other**.

The more circles there are, and the closer they are together, the **higher** the mountain.

A mountain with **two peaks** is represented by well-spaced concentric circles.

Help Tom match the **stickers** with **contour lines** to the corresponding mountains.

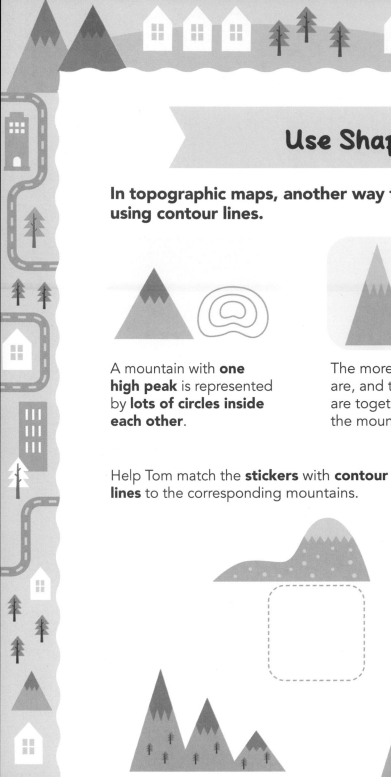

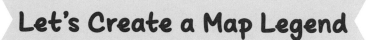

Let's Create a Map Legend

In addition to colors, shapes, and pictures, symbols are also used on maps.

A **legend** is a table that is put on maps to explain the meaning of the symbols that are used. This means that anyone who reads the map can understand everything that is represented. Here are some examples:

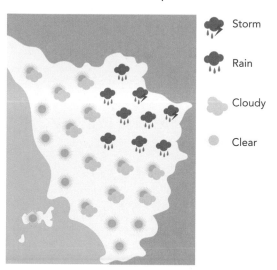

- Storm
- Rain
- Cloudy
- Clear

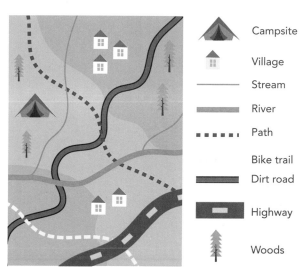

- Campsite
- Village
- Stream
- River
- Path
- Bike trail
- Dirt road
- Highway
- Woods

Gea has to draw a **legend** for the map of her city.
Attach the **stickers** depicting the **symbols** of the features in the city above the correct descriptions.

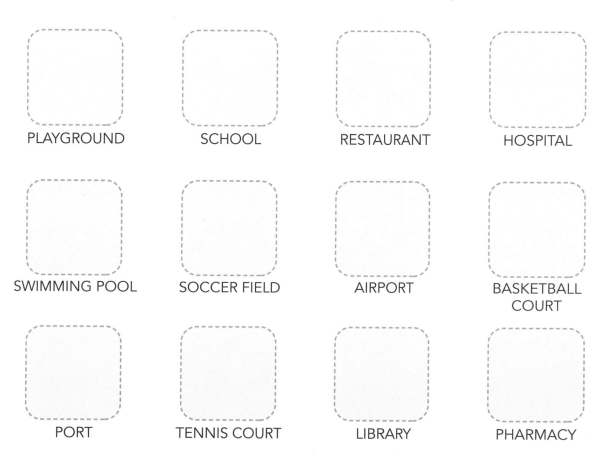

PLAYGROUND   SCHOOL   RESTAURANT   HOSPITAL

SWIMMING POOL   SOCCER FIELD   AIRPORT   BASKETBALL COURT

PORT   TENNIS COURT   LIBRARY   PHARMACY

Turning Pictures into Symbols

Tom is having problems matching the pictures of the places to the symbols they correspond to on the maps.

Help him by attaching the correct **sticker** next to each place, as shown in the example on the right.

    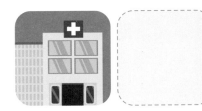

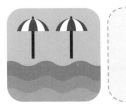     

Let's Play with Symbols

Gea's also not sure about the symbols. Can you help her?

Match the stickers to the places they refer to, as shown in the example.

Complete the Map

Fill in the blank spaces.

Read the **legend** and fill in the blank spaces with the correct stickers, which you can find at the back of the book.

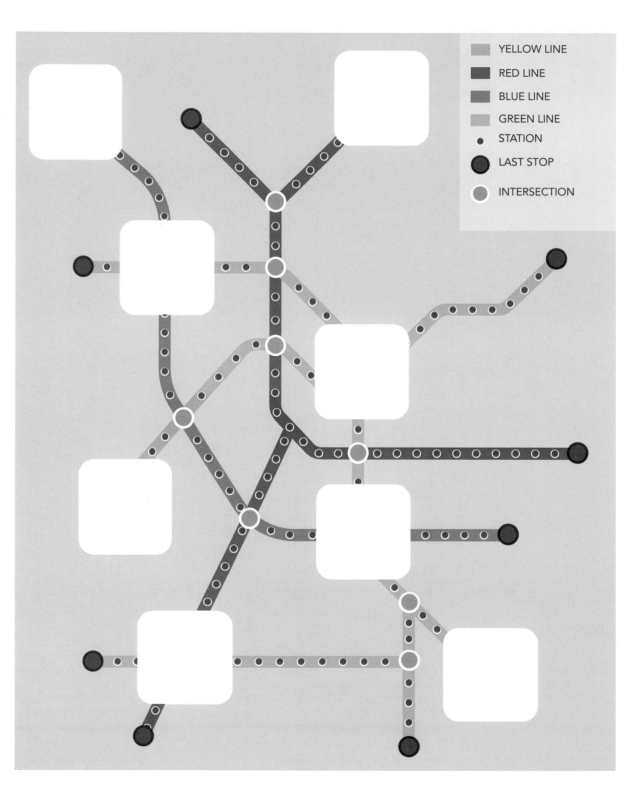

YELLOW LINE

RED LINE

BLUE LINE

GREEN LINE

• STATION

LAST STOP

INTERSECTION

Find the Mistakes

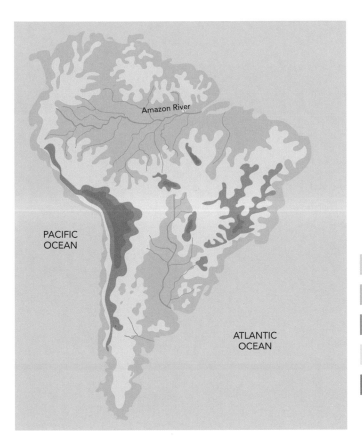

PACIFIC OCEAN

Amazon River

ATLANTIC OCEAN

There are some mistakes in both of these maps.

Now that you know how natural and man-made features are represented, you won't have any problems finding them! Look at the **legends** in both maps very carefully ...

What do you think South America looks like? Choose the correct sticker and attach it here.

PLAIN

SHALLOW SEA

VERY DEEP SEA

HILLS

MOUNTAINS

Some of the locations in the map of the town below are mislabeled. Use the stickers to fix the mistakes.

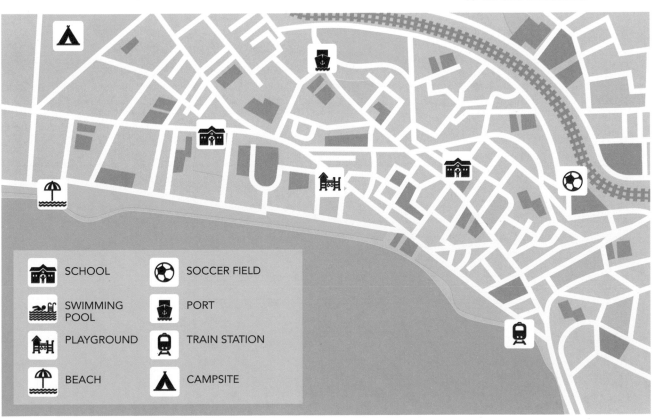

SCHOOL

SWIMMING POOL

PLAYGROUND

BEACH

SOCCER FIELD

PORT

TRAIN STATION

CAMPSITE

Let's Draw a Floor Plan

Floor plans are graphic representations of small spaces, such as an office or a room.

I made a **floor plan** of my **bedroom**.
As you can see from the **legend**, everything in the room is **seen from above**.
Get a piece of paper and try making one yourself, using your ruler and the symbols in the legend!

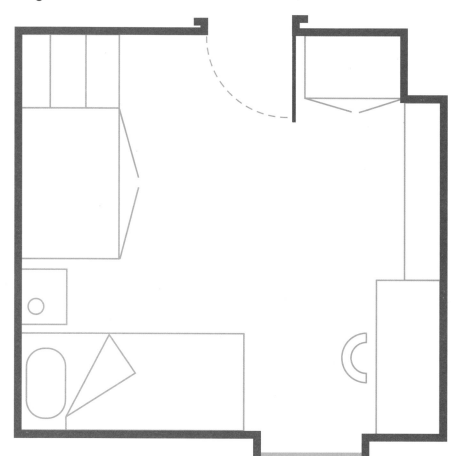

LEGEND

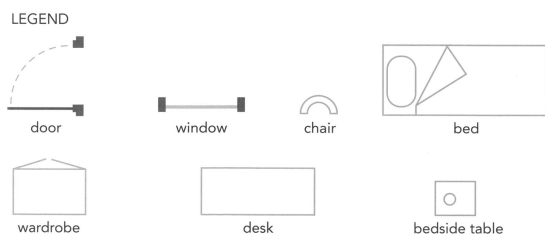

door   window   chair   bed

wardrobe   desk   bedside table

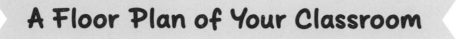

A Floor Plan of Your Classroom

Gea had to make a floor plan of her classroom. She did a good job, didn't she? Would you like to make one of your classroom?

Get a piece of paper and use your ruler and the symbols in Gea's legend to draw the floor plan of your classroom.

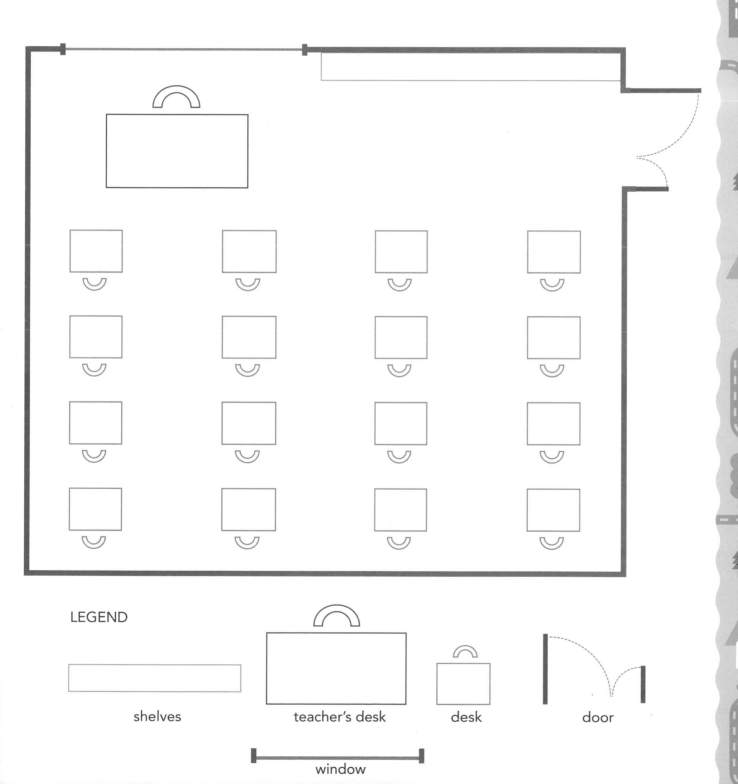

LEGEND

shelves   teacher's desk   desk   door

window

The Apprentice Cartographer Quiz

**We now know a lot about how maps are made.
See if you can answer the following questions.
Use the pages of the book to help if you don't know the answer!**

- The word "geography" means "**a description of the earth**" . . . . T F

- **Cartography** is the science of making geographical maps . . . . T F

- There is only one type of map . . . . T F

- A **globe** shows us the whole planet on a flat piece of paper . . . . T F

- The **cardinal points** make it possible for us to orient ourselves . . . . T F

- A magnetic **compass** always points east . . . . T F

- The **sun** rises in the **east** and sets in the **west** . . . . T F

- A map grid is a grid . . . . T F

- The method for reproducing smaller versions of large surface areas is called "**scaling up**" . . . . T F

Congratulations! You are now an apprentice cartographer!

Stick your
rosette here!

Stick your
rosette here!

The Geographical Memory Game

There's nothing better than a game to help you remember everything you have learned! Let's make it together!

Stick the memory card stickers at the back of the book on to a piece of cardboard. There are **21 pairs**, for a total of 42 cards.

Cut them out, carefully cutting along the outlines.

Turn them over without looking at the images and arrange them on a table or surface.

Play with a friend!

Take turns flipping over two tiles; if they are not the same, turn them back over. Then it's the other player's turn.

If a player finds a pair of identical tiles, they keep them and then get another turn; if they don't make a match, it's the other player's turn again.

The game ends when there are no tiles left.

The winner is the person who collected the most pairs!

Solutions

Geography and Its Tools p. 7
Answer: COMPASS

The Cartographer's Quiz p. 8
Answer: MAPS

What's Tom Drawing? p. 9

B I N O C U L A R S
C O M P A S S
B O O K S
M O U N T A I N
P E N C I L
C O M P A S S
R U L E R

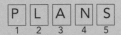

Types of Maps pp. 12-13

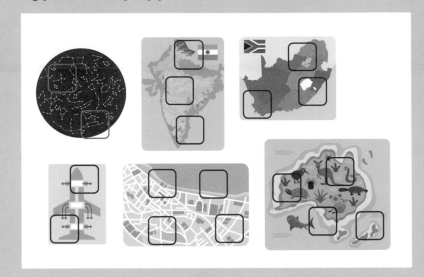

Find the Map pp. 14-15

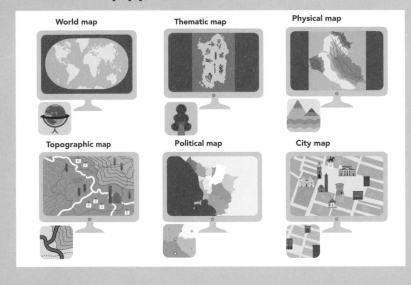

The World Map pp. 16-17

How many **geo-notches** are there between ...

- Gea and the moose? 8

- Gea and polar bear? 12

- Tom and the panda? 9

- The kangaroo and the tiger? 11

- The lion and the crocodile? 12

- The tiger and the panda? 5

- Tom and the lion? 9

- The crocodile and the penguin? 12

Time to Go Home! p. 18

Don't Lose Your Way p. 19

Find the Points pp. 24-25 and 26-27

BEGINNER'S LEVEL Where's the hotel excelsior in relation to Gea? **South**
INTERMEDIATE LEVEL Where's the airport in relation to Tom? **North**
EXPERT LEVEL Where's the hospital in relation to Gea? **West**
FINAL CHALLENGE Where's the tower in relation to Tom? **Northeast**

Ready, Set, Go! p. 31

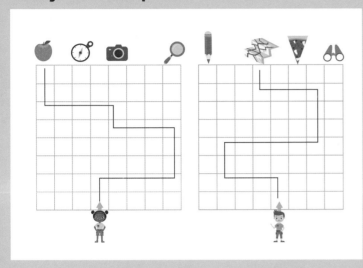

How to Use a Map Grid p. 32

Where's the **flower**? **B1**

Where's the **chestnut**? **F2**

Where's the **stone**? **E7**

Where's the **mushroom**? **B6**

Where's the **ladybug**? **A3**

Where's the **tree**? **D5**

Where's the **pine cone**? **E4**

How to Use a Map Grid p. 33

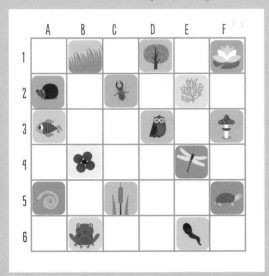

Let's Scale Down p. 37

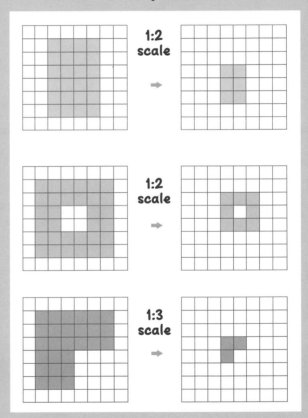

Natural and Artificial Features p. 38

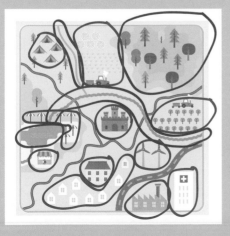

A Matter of Colors p. 39

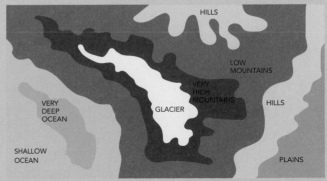

Let's Play with Pictures pp. 40-41

*The positions of the stickers within each map may vary.

Use Shapes p. 42

Let's Create a Map Legend p. 43

PLAYGROUND

SCHOOL

RESTAURANT

SWIMMING POOL

SOCCER FIELD

AIRPORT

PORT

TENNIS COURT

LIBRARY

HOSPITAL

BASKETBALL COURT

PHARMACY

Turning Pictures Into Symbols p. 44

Let's Play with Symbols p. 45

Complete the Map p. 46

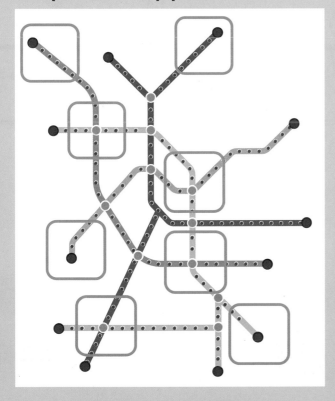

Find the Mistakes p. 47

The Apprentice Cartographer Quiz p. 50

- The word "geography" means "a description of the earth" **T**
- **Cartography** is the science of making geographical maps **T**
- There is only one type of map **F**
- A **globe** shows us the whole planet on a flat piece of paper **F**
- The **cardinal points** make it possible for us to orient ourselves **T**
- A magnetic **compass** always points east **F**
- The **sun** rises in the **east** and sets in the **west T**
- A map grid is a grid **T**
- The method for reproducing smaller versions of large surface areas is called "**scaling up**" **F**

Paola Misesti

Paola was born in Como, Italy, in 1970, and has been living in Zurich, Switzerland, with her family since 2011. She is an educator who teaches Italian to foreign students, and she has also written and cowritten educational creativity and design books. She has trained educators, teachers, and parents for many years and does workshops and educational projects in kindergartens and elementary schools. For the past 10 years, she has been sharing her experiences and materials online, on her website *homemademamma.com*.

Agnese Baruzzi

Agnese has a degree in graphic design from ISIA (Institute of Higher Education in the Artistic Industries), in Urbino, Italy. Since 2001, she has been working as an illustrator and author. She has created numerous children's books in both Italy and abroad. She holds workshops for children and adults, collaborating with schools and libraries. In recent years, she has beautifully illustrated several books for White Star Kids.

White Star Kids™ is a trademark of White Star s.r.l.

© 2022 White Star s.r.l.
Piazzale Luigi Cadorna, 6
20123 Milan, Italy
www.whitestar.it

Originally published in 2022 as *Mad for Geography—Maps* by White Star, this North American version titled *All About Maps Amazing Activity Book* is published in 2023 by Fox Chapel Publishing Company, Inc. Reproduction of its contents is strictly prohibited without written permission from the rights holder.

Happy Fox Books is an imprint of Fox Chapel Publishing Company, Inc., 903 Square Street, Mount Joy, PA 17552.

ISBN 978-1-64124-331-5

To learn more about the other great books from Fox Chapel Publishing, or to find a retailer near you, call toll-free 800-457-9112 or visit us at *www.FoxChapelPublishing.com*.

We are always looking for talented authors.
To submit an idea, please send a brief inquiry to acquisitions@foxchapelpublishing.com.

Printed in China
First Printing

PP. 12-13: TYPES OF MAPS

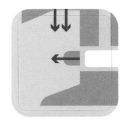

PP. 14-15: FIND THE MAP

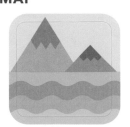

PP. 16-17: THE WORLD MAP: EARTH AT A GLANCE

PP. 32-33: HOW TO USE A MAP GRID

PP. 40-41: LET'S PLAY WITH PICTURES

 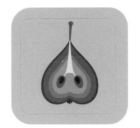  

P. 42: USE SHAPES

P. 42: USE SHAPES

P. 43: LET'S CREATE A MAP LEGEND

P. 44: TURNING PICTURES INTO SYMBOLS

P. 45: LET'S PLAY WITH SYMBOLS

P. 46: COMPLETE THE MAP

P. 47: FIND THE MISTAKES

P. 47: FIND THE MISTAKES

P. 50: GEO ROSETTES

P. 51: THE GEOGRAPHICAL MEMORY GAME